Rivers

Nicola Edwards

WAYLAND

eography First

Titles in this series
Coasts • Islands • Maps and Symbols
Mountains • Rivers • Volcanoes

© 2004 White-Thomson Publishing Ltd

Produced for Hodder Wayland by
White-Thomson Publishing Ltd
2/3 St Andrew's Place
Lewes, East Sussex
BN7 1UP

Geography consultant: John Lace, School Adviser
Editor: Katie Orchard
Picture research: Glass Onion Pictures
Designer: Chris Halls at Mind's Eye Design, Lewes
Artist: Peter Bull

Published in Great Britain in 2004 by Hodder Wayland,
an imprint of Hodder Children's Books.

This paperback edition published in 2006 by Wayland,
an imprint of Hachette Children's Books.

The right of Nicola Edwards to be identified as the
author has been asserted by her in accordance with
the Copyright, Designs and Patents Act 1988.

British Library Cataloguing in Publication Data
Edward, Nicola
   Rivers and Streams. - (Geography First)
   Rivers - Juvenile literature
   I. Title II. Orchard, Katie
   551.4'83

ISBN-10: 0 7502 4632 4
ISBN-13: 978 0 7502 4632 3

Printed in China

Wayland
An imprint of Hachette Children's Books
338 Euston Road, London NW1 3BH

Cover: A boat on the James River, Virginia, USA.
Title page: A view of the River Rhine, in Germany.
Futher information page: The spectacular Iguacu Falls.

Acknowledgements:
The author and publisher would like to thank the following for their permission to reproduce the following
photographs: Ecoscene 12 (Wayne Lawler), 24 (Eric Schaffer), 25 (Blonfield); Getty Images cover, Hodder
Wayland Picture Library *title page, contents page, chapter openers*, 5 (Gordon Clements), 9, 18, 28, 31;
Oxford Scientific Films 7 (Steffen Hauser), 8 (Ronald Toms), 13 (Ronald Toms), 15 (Paulo de Oliviera), 21
(Norbert Rosing), 26 (Andrew Lister); Still Pictures 10 (Jim Wark), 14 (Mark Carwardine), 16 David Hoffman),
17 (Paul Brown), 19 (Cyril Ruoso), 22 (Shehzad Nooran), 23 (Juntawonsup/UNEP), 27 (Bojan Brecli).

Words in bold **like this** are explained in the glossary on page 30.

Contents

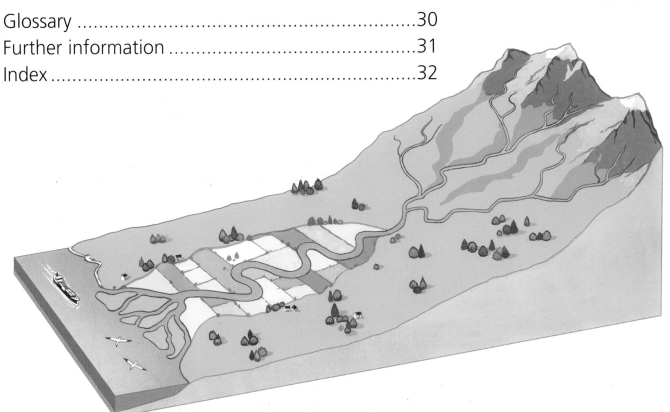

Rivers and change

All living things need water to live and grow. Water is **recycled** and moved around the Earth in a process called the **water cycle**. Rivers and streams play an important part in this cycle.

Streams and rivers come in many sizes, from trickling springs to mighty, raging masses of water.

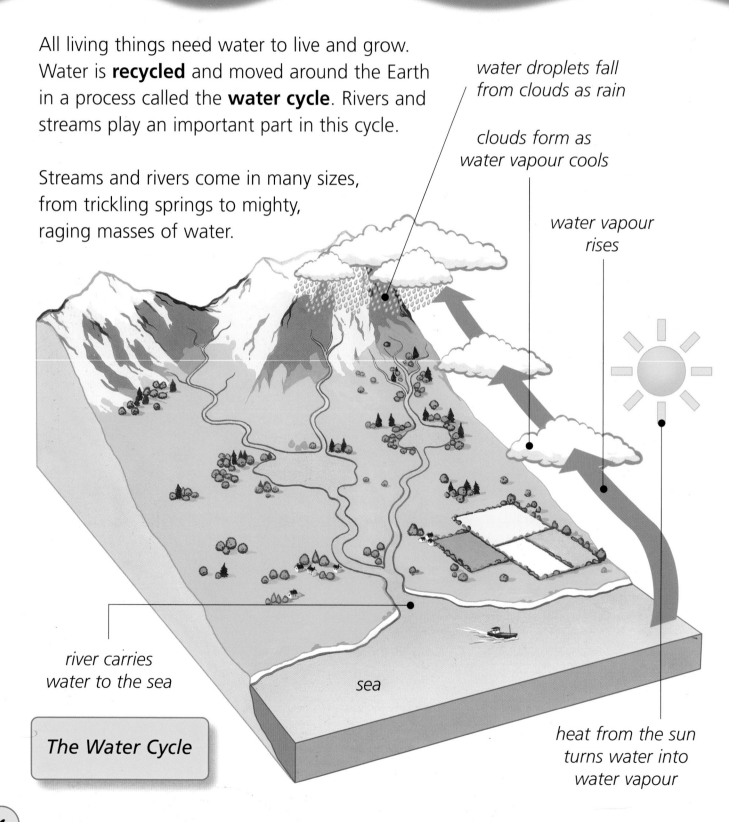

water droplets fall from clouds as rain

clouds form as water vapour cools

water vapour rises

river carries water to the sea

sea

heat from the sun turns water into water vapour

The Water Cycle

They all change the shape of the landscape around them. Moving water wears away material such as gravel and mud, and transports it to new places. The material is **deposited**, or dropped, by rivers and streams as they flow downhill.

▼ A waterfall carves a path to reach a woodland stream.

A river's journey

The start of a river is called its source. High up in hills or mountains, many rivers begin their journey as springs.

Rain falls over the land and runs down into cracks in the rocks. The water bubbles to the surface from underground and trickles out to form a stream. This stream is joined by smaller streams called **tributaries**. Together they form a river.

A River's Journey from Source to Sea

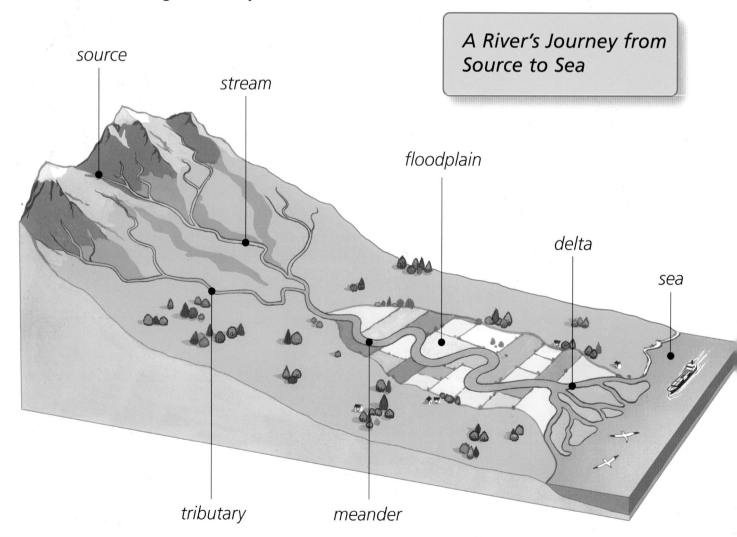

source

stream

floodplain

delta

sea

tributary

meander

The route a river takes is called its course. From its source, a river flows steeply downhill. Over flatter land it may curve in wide loops. Most rivers end their journey at the sea. The place where the water flows into the sea is called the river's **mouth**.

▲ *This stream in Switzerland began its journey high up in the mountains.*

Wearing away the land

At the start of a river's course, the water is shallow. It swirls around a bed of gravel and tumbles over rocks. The rushing water, or **current**, picks up gravel, stones and rocks, and sweeps them along. This is the river's **load**.

If the amount of water in a river increases, for example, after a heavy storm, it can carry an even bigger load.

▼ *The Colorado River cuts into the rock around it, in the Grand Canyon, USA.*

As the river flows, its load scrapes and cuts into the **riverbed**. Over thousands of years it can wear away, or **erode**, the land to form deep-sided, V-shaped **valleys**. Sometimes a river flows over a cliff of hard rock and then gushes down as a waterfall.

▼ *Waterfalls like the Iguaçú Falls, bordering Brazil and Argentina, can be spectacular.*

The floodplain

When a river flowing downhill meets land with a gentler slope, the water flows in wide, snake-like curves. These are called **meanders**. The river is carrying a load of muddy material. The riverbed is lined with smooth silt, which makes it easy for the water to rush over it.

▼ *The Kuskokwim River, USA, meanders across the floodplain.*

After heavy rain, the river may spill out on to the surrounding land, called the **floodplain**. Floodwater deposits stones, sand and mud. These deposits build gradually to form high-sided banks called **levees**.

During a flood, a river can change its course. Sometimes the strong current makes the river cut across a meander. A curved lake, called an **ox-bow lake**, is left behind.

How an Ox-bow Lake is Formed

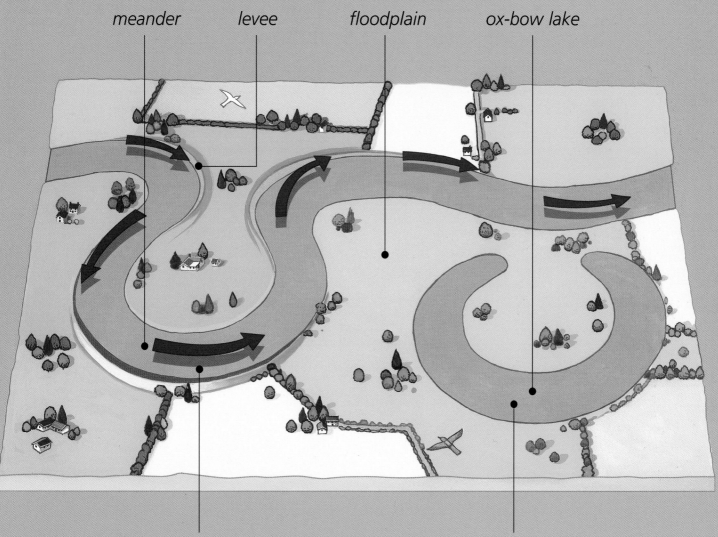

meander   levee   floodplain   ox-bow lake

meander forms a loop

river changes course and cuts off the loop, leaving behind an ox-bow lake

A river meets the sea

By the time a river reaches the sea, its current is much slower and weaker. The river drops more of its load of sand, mud and gravel. This builds up at the river's mouth to form a triangular area of little islands called a **delta**. The river flows around the islands in streams to reach the sea.

▼ *The Burdekin delta opens out to meet the sea, North Queensland, Australia.*

Sometimes a river does not form a delta. Instead its mouth widens until it meets the sea. This is called an **estuary**.

▼ *A fishing boat leaves the mouth of the Rance estuary, in France.*

River wildlife

Rivers and streams are home to all kinds of wildlife, from the tiniest plant to the largest hippos. Many river animals, such as otters and beavers, are fantastic swimmers. Crocodiles can move quickly in and out of the water.

▼ *A brown bear in Alaska catches a salmon as it leaps out of the water.*

Tiny insects such as water beetles and pond skaters live in or on the water. Dragonflies start their lives in the water and leave when they are adult. Fish, such as trout and carp, eat river insects. Fierce pike eat frogs and ducklings that live along the river.

Many birds live around rivers, feeding on plants, insects and fish. Kingfishers live along the riverbank and moorhens build their nests in the reeds at the water's edge.

▲ *A kingfisher dives at high speed to catch a frog.*

Using water from rivers

From the earliest times people have settled and built homes close to rivers. Many towns began as small riverside settlements. Water is needed in homes for drinking, cooking, washing and getting rid of waste.

Water is also important for farming. Rivers carry mud and soil from place to place. When a river floods it deposits a layer of rich, fertile soil on to the floodplain. This makes the land ideal for growing crops.

▲ *People wash their clothes and swim in the River Cuera in Venezuela.*

Farmers may also dig channels to bring river water to the surrounding fields so that they can grow crops. This is called **irrigation**.

▼ *This irrigation channel is fed by water from the River Po, in Italy. This farmer is using a pump to water his crops.*

On the river

Before there were roads or railways, people travelled along rivers to find their way into new places. Rivers connected the settlements along their banks. People built boats and used them to carry goods and passengers from one place to another.

▼ *A group of tourists in Canada rides the rapids.*

Many people enjoy spending their spare time on or around rivers. Streams and rivers often run through areas of beautiful scenery. People enjoy fishing, walking or cycling along riverbanks. Sailing, canoeing and rafting are popular river sports.

◀ *A farmer sells produce from his boat at a floating market in Thailand.*

Power from rivers

The force of water rushing downhill is an important source of energy. **Hydroelectric power stations** use this downward movement of water to make electricity. First, people have to build a **dam** across a river.

A Hydroelectric Power Station

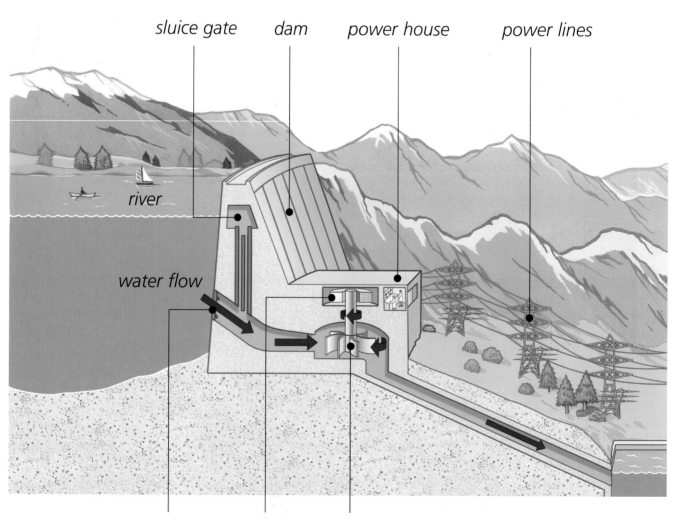

sluice gate   dam   power house   power lines

river

water flow

filter gate   dynamo   turbine

The water builds up behind the dam and this raises the level of water in the river. The water gushes through tunnels and turns huge water wheels called **turbines**. The turbines are connected to machines called **dynamos** that produce electricity.

Power stations are expensive to build, but moving water is a safe and cheap source of energy that will never run out.

▲ *Glen Dam, Arizona, USA. The water used in the power station is pumped back to the river.*

Floods and droughts

After very heavy rain, rivers can flood. A river may change its course, sweeping away everything in its path. Huge amounts of sand and mud, and larger objects such as rocks and trees, can all get washed away.

A serious flood can cause terrible damage to homes and buildings, and people can be killed.

▼ *In 1998 Bangladesh was hit by terrible flooding, leaving many people homeless.*

In times of drought, when there is not enough rain, rivers can dry up, leaving behind a patchwork of cracks in the hard mud. Droughts threaten the lives of people and wildlife that depend on rivers for their survival.

▲ *Many people rely on rivers for water. This river in Thailand has almost dried up.*

River pollution

Many of the world's rivers are being **polluted**. Sewage, factory waste, farming chemicals and oil leaks make river water unsafe for wildlife to live in and dangerous for people to drink.

People who carelessly throw crisp packets, cans and other rubbish into rivers and streams add to the problem.

▼ *Throwing waste into rivers makes the water unfit for wildlife to live in.*

People are now starting to clean up rivers and repair some of the damage. Big companies that own factories near rivers often have to follow rules to make sure they do not pollute the water. Once the water is clean again, wildlife can return to the river.

▲ *These fishermen will not be able to catch any fish in this polluted river for a long time.*

Saving water

Water from rivers and streams is very precious. In parts of the world where it does not rain very much, water is often in short supply. One-fifth of the world's population does not have clean water to drink. These people risk catching diseases such as typhoid and cholera, which are spread by germs in water.

▼ *These children in Zimbabwe are learning how to keep water clean and avoid spreading diseases.*

The vicious circle

It is important not to waste water. In wealthy countries, toilets, showers and washing machines are being designed to use less water than before.

When there has been little rain, people are told to use their bathwater to water their garden, instead of using a hosepipe. In some countries, water that has been used in homes is recycled for use on farms and in factories.

▲ *It is important to make the most of the world's water. This machinery removes salt from seawater so that people can drink it.*

River fact file

1. The Nile, the world's longest river, is 6,695 kilometres long. It is really two rivers, the White Nile and the Blue Nile, which join at Khartoum in the Sudan, in Africa.

2. At 6,436 kilometres, the Amazon River in South America is almost as long as the Nile. Its source is in the Andes Mountains in Peru. The mouth of the river is 270 kilometres wide.

3. North America's longest (and muddiest) river is the Mississippi, which is 3,765 kilometres long.

4. The Ganges in India (below) is a holy river to Hindu people, who come to bathe in it.

5. The Huang He, or Yellow River, in China gets its name from the huge amount of sand and mud that it carries, turning the water a yellowy-brown colour.

6. Australia's longest river is the Murray. It is 2,589 kilometres long.

7. The longest river in Europe is the Volga, which flows for 3,685 kilometres through Russia. The Danube and the Rhine are also important European rivers. They have been vital to the development of trade and transport throughout Europe.

8. At 75,000 square kilometres, the Ganges–Brahmaputra (in India and Bangladesh) is the largest delta in the world.

9. The highest waterfall in the world, with a drop of 979 metres, is the Angel Falls in Venezuela, South America.

10 The world's worst-ever flood happened around the Bay of Bengal in 1970. Millions of people lost their homes and 500,000 people were killed.

11 China suffered the world's worst drought between 1876 and 1879, when 9 million people died.

Major Rivers of the World

Numbers on this map refer to numbers in the fact file.

Glossary

Current The flow of water in a river.

Dam A structure that is built across a river. Water collects behind a dam.

Delta A triangular area of little islands and streams that is formed by a river as it meets the sea.

Deposit Material that is dropped or left behind by a flowing river.

Dynamo A machine that makes electricity.

Erode Wear away.

Estuary The place where a river mouth opens into the sea.

Floodplain A flat area of land that a river runs through and may flood over.

Hydroelectric power station A power station that turns energy from moving water into electricity.

Irrigation Bringing water from rivers to farmland where crops are grown.

Levees High-sided banks of land formed from material deposited by rivers.

Load Material such as sand, mud and stones carried along by a river.

Meander The curve of a river as it winds across a floodplain.

Mouth The end of a river's course, where it meets the sea.

Ox-bow lake A curved lake formed when a river changes its course and cuts off the loop of a meander.

Polluted Made dirty or unsafe.

Recycled Used again.

Riverbed The bottom of a river.

Tributaries Smaller rivers that join a larger river.

Turbine A huge wheel that is turned by a current of water.

Valley An area of land through which a river flows.

Water cycle The circular process by which water moves continuously around the Earth: from sea to atmosphere, to the Earth's surface and back to the sea.

Further information

Books to Read:

Pond and River (Eyewitness Guides) by Steve Parker (Dorling Kindersley, 2003)

The River Book by Dr Brian Knapp (Atlantic Europe Publishing Company, 2004)

Rivers (Earth in Danger) by Polly Goodman (Hodder Wayland, 2001)

River (Our Earth) by Terry Jennings (Belitha, 1999)

Rivers and Streams (Geography Starts Here!) by Jenny Vaughan (Hodder Wayland, 2001)

Rivers in the Rain Forest by Saviour Pirotta (Hodder Wayland, 1997)

The Water Cycle (Cycles in Nature) by Theresa Greenaway (Hodder Wayland, 2000)

Index

All the numbers in **bold** refer to photographs and illustrations as well as text.